BUENOS AIR

THE CITY AT A GLANCE

CW00732345

El Obelisco

Part monument, part mascot, this
concrete-and-stone spike was desi
the modernist architect Alberto Prebisch.
It went up in just 31 days in 1936.
Avenida Corrientes/Avenida 9 de Julio

Casa Rosada

Government House acquired its pink hue in
the late 1860s and its Italianate archway in
1890. President Fernando de la Rúa fled the
country from the roof by helicopter in 2001.
Balcarce 50, T 4344 3804

Banco Hipotecario

Architect Clorindo Testa made his name
with this massive, Meccano-like bank HQ.
See p035

ARA Presidente Sarmiento

The English-built frigate served as the
Argentine navy's training vessel between
1897 and 1960. It's now a floating museum.
Ave Alicia Moreau de Justo 980, T 4334 9386

Puente de la Mujer

Santiago Calatrava's graceful 2001 bridge is
much loved by (hard-to-please) porteños.
See p074

Edificio Kavanagh

At 120m, the Kavanagh became the highest
reinforced-concrete structure in Latin America
in 1936. Combining elements of art deco and
rationalism, it possesses an austere beauty.
See p012

Catalinas Norte

This high-rise cluster went up between 1972
and 2001. Several were designed by locals,
including Cesar Pelli's Torre BankBoston and
Mario Roberto Álvarez's Torre IBM (see p013).

INTRODUCTION
THE CHANGING FACE OF THE URBAN SCENE

As 21st-century BA hits its stride, this thrilling city – part heritage site, part urban sprawl – remains hard to pin down. We can spot some persistent motifs, of course. The architecture that looks as if it leapt from the pages of a coffee-table book; the social scene that runs from laidback gatherings sharing yerba maté in the park to branded polo parties in made-over palazzos; the blend of cool and approachability that makes locals so appealing; and yes, the steak and the wine, the absurdly late nights and a thriving cocktail culture. People have always adored these aspects, and long may they reign.

Step off the tourist trail, however, and you'll find a capital in flux. As the country's notorious boom-and-bust cycle seems to be finally flattening out, Argentines who once would have sought fortunes abroad are staying put – or coming back. They are overhauling the infrastructure, opening art galleries and curating exhibitions, and harbouring ambitions to challenge Peru's status as the continent's culinary king with a grassroots *nueva cocina argentina* movement. These currents join what is already a mighty river of creativity, from the venerable architects Clorindo Testa and Cesar Pelli, and bold developers like Alan Faena, to the kids with cans who have created a street-art mecca. This is still a developing city, where policemen smoke on duty and commuters hang out of train doors, but BA is cleaner and safer than it has been in years. If porteños can add civic pride to their long list of virtues, there may be no stopping them.

ESSENTIAL INFO

FACTS, FIGURES AND USEFUL ADDRESSES

TOURIST OFFICE
Avenida Quintana 596
T 4806 0904
www.turismo.buenosaires.gob.ar

TRANSPORT
Airport transfer to city centre
www.tiendaleon.com
The bus journey takes about an hour
Car hire
Avis
T 4480 9387
Metro
www.buenosaires.gob.ar/subte
Trains run from 5am until about 10.30pm
Taxis
Premier Radio Taxi
T 4858 0888
Call for a cab. Avoid unmarked taxis
Travel card
www.sube.gob.ar

EMERGENCY SERVICES
Ambulance
T 107
Fire
T 100
Police
T 911
24-hour pharmacy
Florida 474
T 4322 6435

EMBASSIES
British Embassy
Dr Luis Agote 2412
T 4808 2200
www.gov.uk/government/world/argentina
US Embassy
Avenida Colombia 4300
T 5777 4533
ar.usembassy.gov

POSTAL SERVICES
Post office
Correo Argentino
Teniente General Juan Domingo Perón 321
T 4891 9191
Shipping
UPS
T 0800 2222 877

BOOKS
Blow-Up and Other Stories by Julio
Cortázar (Random House)
Clorindo Testa: Architect edited by
Kristin Feireiss (NAI Publishers)
Textura Dos: Buenos Aires Street Art
by Guilherme Zauith and Matthew
Fox-Tucker (Mark Batty Publisher)

WEBSITES
Art
www.artealdia.com
www.malba.org.ar
Newspaper
www.buenosairesherald.com

EVENTS
arteBA
www.arteba.com
Casa FOA
www.casafoa.com

COST OF LIVING
Taxi from Ezeiza Airport to city centre
ARS650
Cappuccino
ARS45
Packet of cigarettes
ARS30
Daily newspaper
ARS15
Bottle of champagne
ARS250

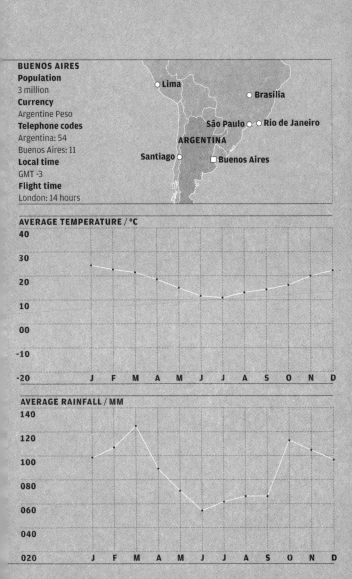

BUENOS AIRES
Population
3 million
Currency
Argentine Peso
Telephone codes
Argentina: 54
Buenos Aires: 11
Local time
GMT -3
Flight time
London: 14 hours

Lima

Brasília

São Paulo   Rio de Janeiro

ARGENTINA

Santiago   Buenos Aires

AVERAGE TEMPERATURE / °C

| | J | F | M | A | M | J | J | A | S | O | N | D |

40
30
20
10
00
-10
-20

AVERAGE RAINFALL / MM

| | J | F | M | A | M | J | J | A | S | O | N | D |

140
120
100
080
060
040
020

NEIGHBOURHOODS
THE AREAS YOU NEED TO KNOW AND WHY

To help you navigate the city, we've chosen the most interesting districts (see below and the map inside the back cover) and colour-coded our featured venues, according to their location; those venues that are outside these areas are not coloured.

LA BOCA

At the turn of the 20th century, La Boca, the true cradle of tango, was a flourishing port district settled by Genoese immigrants. It was neglected for decades but projects like edgy art space Fundación Proa (see p058) signal a revival. La Bombonera (Brandsen 805, T 4309 4700), home to Boca Juniors, is one of the world's great sporting venues.

SAN TELMO

Cobblestones, old churches and crumbling stucco facades give San Telmo an if-these-walls-could-talk feel that draws in tourists, artists and street performers. Hip hotels have now opened here (see p016), and the Sunday market in Plaza Dorrego, which stretches along Calle Defensa, is popular.

PALERMO

BA's largest 'hood, Palermo, comprises various unofficial sub-barrios, including Bosques de Palermo (botanical gardens and parks), Palermo Chico, with its expats, embassies and celebs, and swanky Las Cañitas, home to the polo ground (Avenida del Libertador 4300, T 4576 5600).

MICROCENTRO

The chaotic city centre fans out from Plaza de Mayo and the pink presidential palace, Casa Rosada (Balcarce 50, T 4344 3804), which was inaugurated in 1862. Attractions abound, from the sumptuous late 19th-century architecture of Avenida de Mayo to the world-class Teatro Colón (see p009).

PUERTO MADERO

Thanks to an ambitious regeneration programme that commenced in the early 1990s, the old dockland is now one of the city's smartest neighbourhoods. On the west side (completed), you'll find pricey, business-oriented restaurants; on the east (ongoing), luxury hotels and flashy skyscrapers such as Torre YPF (see p015).

RECOLETA

This district's mansard apartment blocks, designer boutiques, tree-flanked avenues and ladies who lunch (often with their toy dogs) helped give the city its chic rep. The famous cemetery (see p034) is ringed by five-star hotels (see p016) and mansions that were built during BA's golden age.

PALERMO VIEJO

Old Palermo is further divided into Soho and Hollywood; the former characterised by fashion and homewares boutiques, the latter by TV/film studios. It's packed with happening bars and eateries like Ninina (see p025) and Tegui (see p047), but rents are rising and the chains are moving in.

RETIRO

With a clocktower that resembles Big Ben (Torre Monumental), a railway station that evokes St Pancras (Retiro) and plazas and buildings that bring to mind Paris or Madrid, Retiro bears a heavy stamp of European influences. However, Edificio Kavanagh (see p012) is a true original.

LANDMARKS
THE SHAPE OF THE CITY SKYLINE

This is a sprawling, not soaring city. Unlike, say, Manhattan, you can understand Buenos Aires without ever seeing it from the air. Its mansions, cafés and plazas dominate urban mythology here in a way that high-rises and pharaonic monuments never could: El Obelisco (Plaza de la República), constructed in 1936 to honour the city's 400th year, is widely loathed. Even BA's most grandiose public work, the 12-lane Avenida 9 de Julio, the first stretch of which was begun in 1935, is a triumph in two dimensions – like the pampas, it impresses through its sheer enormity.

The landmarks that *do* capture the porteño imagination inspire affection rather than awe. The Floralis Genérica (see p068) is an unusually sweet-tempered contemporary sculpture, and Torre YPF (see p015) has earned plaudits for its winter garden. Other, less vainglorious landmarks show the influence of global architectural movements over parochial triumphalism. Edificio Kavanagh (see p012) is a touchstone of rationalism in the Americas; Palacio Barolo (Avenida de Mayo 1370, T 4381 1885), a 1923 proto-skyscraper, is sui generis, but its curves evoke Gaudí and Catalan modernism. The Barolo is one of the buildings to benefit from a refurbishment drive to mark the bicentenary of independence in 2010 – the most comprehensive makeover was reserved for the 1908 Teatro Colón (Cerrito 628, T 4378 7100), now restored to its neoclassical pomp. *For full addresses, see Resources.*

Biblioteca Nacional

Plans for the headquarters of the National
Library were drawn up in 1961 by Clorindo
Testa, during writer Jorge Luis Borges' long
tenure as the institute's director. However,
the complicated techniques needed for its
construction, and dwindling funds, meant
that it took three decades to complete (it
was finished in 1992). Dominating Plaza
Rubén Darío (previously the site of Unzué
Palace, the official Perón residence), it
has been compared to a tree. The millions
of books are kept at root level, protected
from temperature and light fluctuations,
whereas the airy, sunlit reading rooms are
set in the overhanging upper structure,
which is designed to maximise the public
space underneath. Sadly, elements of the
interior are compromised by the fact that
the architects – Testa, Alicia D Cazzanica
and Francisco Bullrich – weren't consulted
during the final stages of the build.
Agüero 2502, T 4808 6000, www.bn.gov.ar

Edificio Kavanagh

In the 1930s, heiress Corina Kavanagh literally bet the farm: she sold her country estancias to finance Buenos Aires' first skyscraper. The flats turned out to be a shrewd investment. Architects Gregorio Sánchez, Ernesto Lagos and Luis María de la Torre's 32-storey reinforced-concrete masterpiece was the tallest structure in Latin America when it was completed in 1936. With its function-first aesthetic,

the Kavanagh was also a 120m-high stake through the heart of BA's neoclassical and Beaux Arts traditions, although its tenants were as happy with the air conditioning (a luxury at the time) as with the rationalist symmetry. The oft-told tale that Kavanagh commissioned the building to spoil the view of her neighbours, the aristocratic Anchorena family, should be true, but isn't. *Florida 1065*

Torre IBM

In the late 1960s, IBM Argentina procured a plot of land in Retiro as part of a state initiative to regenerate the dockside area. The commission was secured by MSGSSS, which included lauded Argentine architects Justo Solsona and Rafael Viñoly, yet the project was stymied due to political unrest. It was revived in 1978, with Mario Roberto Álvarez reworking the proposal as a single edifice that resembles a pile of dominos, completed five years later. He shunned the ubiquitous curtain wall on environmental grounds, and the tower's cantilevered main volume, supported by two central pillars, allows for open-plan interiors, optimising natural light. It might be reminiscent of the Olivetti buildings in Frankfurt, yet Álvarez had created a similar concept two decades earlier for the Banco de Avellaneda.
Ingeniero Enrique Butty 275

Edificio del Ministerio de Salud

Like the woman it depicts, the mural of Eva Perón added to the old Ministerio de Obras Públicas in 2011 is both loved and hated, and nearly impossible to ignore, due to its commanding position on Avenida 9 de Julio, one of the world's busiest roads. The artwork, which measures 31m by 24m, was designed by Eduardo Santoro and built using Corten steel by sculptor Alejandro Marmo, who created an identically sized piece on the opposite side. They capture the first lady in contrasting moods: smiley regal Evita to the south (above); demagogic Evita to the north. Peronist ex-president Cristina Fernández de Kirchner unveiled the work to mark (somewhat randomly) the 59th anniversary of the icon's death, and it is perhaps no coincidence that the shouty side faces Recoleta's upper classes.
Avenida 9 de Julio 1925

Torre YPF

Unveiled in 2008, Cesar Pelli's 160m-high, 36-floor office tower is located in Puerto Madero, the brownfield regeneration site that is BA's skyscraper alley (its neighbour, the 170m Torres El Faro, was designed by Dujovne-Hirsch & Asociados). Torre YPF's irregular facades – one side is rhomboid and angular, the other is curvilinear and smooth – create a sense of horizontal flow coupled with a vertical thrust, as if the structure were the billowing sail of some colossal yacht (appropriate, given that it looks out over the River Plate). Most strikingly, the small forest of eucalyptus trees in the enclosed winter garden on floors 26 to 31 is visible from ground level. Long based in the USA, Pelli may well be Argentina's greatest living architect, and has redefined skylines all over the world.
Macacha Güemes/Juana Manso

HOTELS

WHERE TO STAY AND WHICH ROOMS TO BOOK

Given that every other new hotel in Buenos Aires likes to brand itself as boutique, it can be hard to sort the wheat from the chaff. Palermo Viejo remains the favourite district for savvy travellers; here, Home (see p018) and Fierro (see p022) continue to delight, and more recent arrivals, such as Hotel Clásico (Costa Rica 5480, T 4773 2353) from chef-turned-hotelier Adolfo Suaya, and Legado Mítico (Gurruchaga 1848, T 4833 1300), are keeping them on their toes. For white-gloved service, head to Palacio Duhau Park Hyatt (see p021), Alvear Palace (Avenida Alvear 1891, T 4808 2100) or the Four Seasons (Posadas 1086, T 4321 1200), which underwent a facelift in 2013. More intimate lodgings including MIO (Avenida Quintana 465, T 5295 8500), Hub Porteño (Rodríguez Peña 1967, T 4815 6100) and Algodon Mansion (Montevideo 1647, T 3530 7777) offer five-star amenities without the corporate feel.

Elsewhere, properties in recycled buildings such as Moreno (see p020) and Mansión Vitraux (Carlos Calvo 369, T 4300 6886) draw urbanites to San Telmo, and the Philippe Starck-designed Faena (Marta Salotti 445, T 4010 9000) remains the bobo choice. Chic aparthotels Lemon (Chacabuco 1072, T 4307 5651) and The Haig (Humboldt 2060, T 4772 3761) have outdoor pools, and Oasis (www.oasiscollections.com) has luxury rental addresses across the city, as well as rooms in its hip Clubhouse (Costa Rica, T 4832 5276). *For full addresses and room rates, see Resources.*

Hotel Pulitzer

Catalan Lázaro Rosa-Violán's design for the Pulitzer has made most of its competitors in the CBD look staid. Opened in 2011, its 104 rooms impress with details such as handcrafted bedside tables and lapacho wood minibars by Contemporain Studio, and Suites 1104 and 1204 (above) provide a lesson in loft living. Public spaces borrow icons from decades past and bring them bang up to date – the black-lacquered reception desk gives a nod to the 1930s and blue velvet chesterfields in the bar conjure up 1970s New York. The outdoor eighth-floor pool is an ideal spot for a pre-dinner cool down, and the 13th-floor Sky Bar blends clean Scandinavian lines with lush greenery, and hosts live music in the evenings on Wednesdays and Thursdays.
Maipú 907, T 4316 0800,
www.hotelpulitzer.com.ar

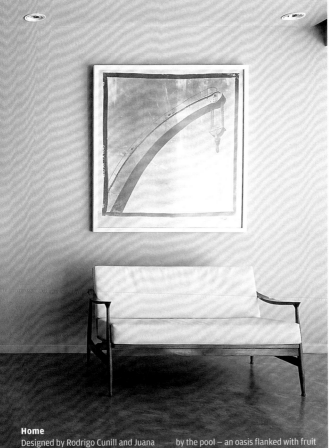

Home

Designed by Rodrigo Cunill and Juana Grichener, Home set the bar high for BA boutique hotels (lobby, pictured) when it opened in 2005. The 20 stylish rooms feature handwoven rugs, William Morris wallpaper and retro furnishings, such as Florence Knoll sofas and George Nelson desks. A pair of lofts have patios fitted with *parrillas* (BBQ grills), and the airy Garden Suite has a roof terrace. Brunch by the pool – an oasis flanked with fruit and jasmine trees – is best enjoyed with a cocktail; the Voy Contigo is made using rum, strawberries, mint and lime. Begin your stay with a trip to the bijou spa for the Jet Lag Recovery treatment, which includes a bath with algae extracts and mineral salts, followed by a massage.
Honduras 5680, T 4778 1008,
www.homebuenosaires.com

Moreno Hotel

A short walk from Microcentro, San Telmo and Puerto Madero, the Moreno is housed in one of the city's finest art deco buildings, which was designed in 1929 by German-Hungarian architect Johannes Kronfuss. It was restored by Fernández, Huberman and Otero in 2007, and boasts a stone-and-tile facade and a flavour of central Europe. The caged lifts and tiled stairwells lead you past some original stained-glass windows into communal areas that are half-Gatsby, half-gaucho. The 37 double-height rooms are surprisingly large and many of them have stunning views of the Basílica de San Francisco; we like to hunker down in one of the Big Lofts (above) with a terrace. The Bebop Music Club (T 4331 3409), situated in the basement, hosts intimate jazz gigs.
Moreno 376, T 6091 2000,
www.morenobuenosaires.com

Palacio Duhau Park Hyatt

This hotel broke the mould for five-star properties in Recoleta when it opened in 2006. Palacio Duhau is refined, but also rigorously contemporary, and forgoes the extravagant flourishes that characterise the neighbourhood's other luxury options. Architects Caparra Entelman & Asociados were responsible for both the new wing and the conversion of the existing 1934 palace (lobby, above), which was designed by Frenchman León Dourge and formerly the home of the aristocratic Duhau family. The signature Hyatt colour palette is used throughout the establishment, enhanced by the occasional flash of a pumpkin-hued wall or crimson throw. The ceiling above the 25m indoor pool features a Barrisol lighting system that simulates daylight. *Avenida Alvear 1661, T 5171 1234, www.buenosaires.park.hyatt.com*

Fierro Hotel

The Fierro has definitely been touched by the zeitgeist – it loans iPads to guests, and a seven-course tasting menu with wine pairings is served at farm-to-fork restaurant UCO (T 3220 6820). Yet this eight-floor property, which has 27 slick, spacious rooms kitted out with black-marble tables, walnut furnishings and works by Argentine artist Jan Kislo, is neither aggressively avant-garde nor preciously hip. Indeed, despite being located within stumbling distance of much of Palermo Hollywood's nightlife, its double-glazed windows, blackout curtains, and discreet heated whirlpool with adjacent sauna distinguish Fierro as something of a haven from the party, rather than being an extension of it.
Soler 5862, T 3220 6800, www.fierrohotel.com

24 HOURS

SEE THE BEST OF THE CITY IN JUST ONE DAY

In this chapter we outline a sensible itinerary that begins at breakfast and ends on the dancefloor. However, Buenos Aires is not a sensible city. You could just as easily start your day at 2.30am, when porteños begin to drift club-wards. Try State (Alsina 940, T 4331 3231) for house and beautiful people, or The Bow (Punta Carrasco, T 4778 1500) for house and... beautiful people. Crash an after-party or go watch the sun rise over the River Plate on the Costanera Norte. Then it's brunch at Fifí Almacén (see p041) or, if it's a Sunday, join the pilgrimage to Malvón (Serrano 789, T 4774 2563). Take a siesta. If you wake up in a *telo*, or 'love' motel, like Dissors (Avenida General Paz 900, T 4653 0314) – aimed at design-conscious hedonists – you'll know you're having a good day.

Hit the galleries in the late afternoon – either an institution such as Museo Nacional de Bellas Artes (Avenida del Libertador 1473, T 5288 9900) or a cool independent like Galería Mar Dulce (Uriarte 1490, T 155 319 3597). Tea at the Alvear Palace Hotel (see p016) might lead to cold beers at La Biela (Avenida Quintana 596, T 4804 0449) and before you know it, you'll be on the vintage malbec at plush Gran Bar Danzón (Libertad 1161, T 4811 1108) or ensconced on the marble stairs, basil daiquiri in hand, at Milion (Paraná 1048, T 4815 9925). Go dance some more at Jet (Avenida Rafael Obligado 4801, T 4782 5599). Sleep is for gringos, after all. *For full addresses, see Resources.*

09.00 Ninina

Emmanuel Paglayan established this airy bakery and café, which has the feel of a chic canteen, in 2013. The interiors are by Estudio Verardo and meld white ceramic wall tiles with oak flooring, stainless steel, copper lights and Thonet chairs. Stop by at any time of day for a meal — waffles and organic fruits for breakfast, or a salad of burrata, prosciutto and sundried tomatoes at lunch, for example — but it is the cakes and pastries that create the queues. A 14m-long Italian marble counter displays mounds of sweet treats, such as traditional *alfajorcitos* biscuits, filled with dulce de leche, or a dairy-free *panneforte*, rich with almonds, raisins and candied orange peel. Paglayan's mother is a fine baker too; the brownie and Linzertorte are her recipes.
Gorriti 4738, T 4832 0070,
www.ninina.com

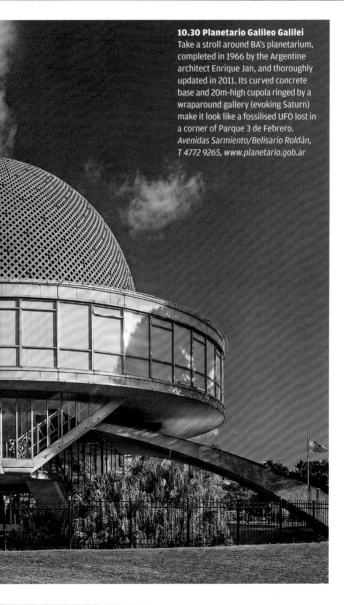

10.30 Planetario Galileo Galilei
Take a stroll around BA's planetarium, completed in 1966 by the Argentine architect Enrique Jan, and thoroughly updated in 2011. Its curved concrete base and 20m-high cupola ringed by a wraparound gallery (evoking Saturn) make it look like a fossilised UFO lost in a corner of Parque 3 de Febrero.
Avenidas Sarmiento/Belisario Roldán, T 4772 9265, www.planetario.gob.ar

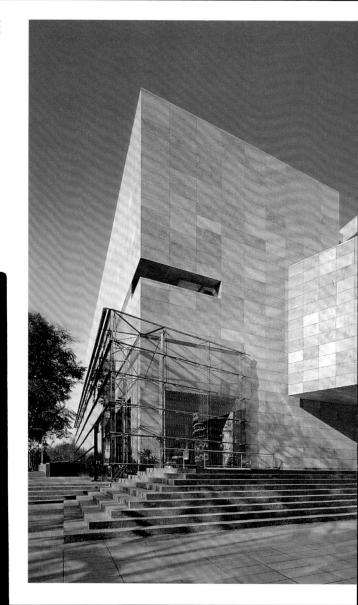

11.15 Malba

This 2001 museum complex is the creation of property tycoon Eduardo F Costantini, one of the world's foremost investors in 20th-century Latin American art. Malba's permanent collection includes works by Antonio Berni, Frida Kahlo, Diego Rivera, Tarsila do Amaral and Xul Solar, and the headline-grabbing temporary shows have featured Andy Warhol and Tracey Emin. There is also an arthouse cinema, a café/restaurant (T 4806 1102) overseen by Marcelo Piégari, and a marvellous shop, Tiendamalba (T 4808 6550), which sells objects by local designers (we liked the tableware by Villa Crespo-based La Feliz). The structure itself, which is clad in Jura limestone, was devised by architects AFT; the intersecting geometric blocks show the influence of Álvaro Siza Vieira, as well as Richard Meier. Closed on Tuesdays.
Avenida Presidente Figueroa Alcorta 3415, T 4808 6500, www.malba.org.ar

13.00 Casa Cavia

You could spend your entire day enjoying the delights of Casa Cavia – it comprises a restaurant, cocktail bar, patisserie, florist, perfumery and publishing house. Built in 1927 as a private home, the property was updated in 2015 by London-based firm KallosTurin, who introduced sleek elements like terrazzo floors and marble counters, along with 'Bertoia Side Chairs'. The flower shop, Flores Pasión, opens directly onto the courtyard, which is flanked by Fueguia 1833 (see p092) and the bar; helmed by Inés de los Santos, it's ideal for an aperitif. A tiny bookshop (above) carries titles by in-house avant-garde imprint Ampersand. Have lunch in the elegant dining space, which serves Pablo Massey's Euro-centric dishes, such as rib-eye with a creamy mash.
Cavia 2985, T 4801 9693,
www.casacavia.com

14.30 8th Spa

This refined urban escape secreted away halfway up the MIO hotel (see p016) offers tantalising glimpses of Cementerio de la Recoleta (overleaf). Covered top to toe in grey slate from the province of San Luis, its defining feature is a 12m-long jacuzzi (right), which is cleverly lit from above and underwater, leaving the impression that you're taking a dip in a candlelit cave. The spa also encompasses a chic steam room, cardio equipment and two massage suites providing de-stressing, relaxing and invigorating treatments – the wine therapy facial is a signature. Gents should pay a visit to the nearby Markus Day Spa For Men (T 4811 0058), which is all blondwood and oak, for a hot shave and haircut, sports massage or, simply, a proper BA preening.
Avenida Quintana 465, T 5295 8500,
www.miobuenosaires.com

8TH SPA

16.00 Cementerio de la Recoleta

One of the most famous cemeteries in the world, Recoleta was first laid out in 1822. But it wasn't until the 1880s, under the direction of architect Juan Buschiazzo, that the necropolis began to take on its current aspect, with the addition of a fluted Doric entrance portico, ever more decorative crypts, and a grid of paved, tree-lined streets that reinforce the sense of a city within a city. Anyone who used to be anyone is buried here, from boxer Luis Ángel Firpo to writer Victoria Ocampo and former president Raúl Alfonsín. Eva Perón, who once said she'd like to bomb Recoleta (the neighbourhood, not the graveyard), is buried inside a black-marble tomb designed to deter grave robbers and (allegedly) withstand a nuclear strike.

Junín 1790, T 4803 1594,
www.cementeriorecoleta.com.ar

17.00 Banco Hipotecario

Clorindo Testa made his name while a partner at SEPRA with this 1959 hulk of soft brutalism for the former Banco de Londres. It is muscular and authoritative, as a bank ought to be; a feat in itself, given the irregular corner site. The reinforced concrete facade, with its unexpected kinks and gaping holes, is divisive – many locals say it's ugly – but undeniably fascinating, and you certainly can't ignore it. A pair of vertical slabs, suspended above the main doors like a portcullis, make an imposing statement, but you shouldn't be put off from entering. Inside, it's a joy: a soaring atrium, a sculptural staircase, a series of cantilevered and suspended levels, wooden cladding and flashes of colour, such as bold cherry-red flooring. Note that the foyer is only open from 10am to 3pm on weekdays. *Reconquista 101*

18.30 Usina del Arte

This 1916 red-brick neo-Renaissance-style building, a former power station designed by Juan Chiogna, with a distinctive clock tower added in 1926, was remodelled into a dynamic performing arts centre in 2012. The complex comprises a vast exhibition hall (above) featuring original iron-truss ceilings that is utilised for large-scale installations, such as Argentinian artist Leandro Erlich's optical illusion *Edificio*, and two auditoriums. Engineer Gustavo Basso, of Estudio Quintana, fashioned the 1,700-seat Sala Sinfónica, which hosts the Buenos Aires Philharmonic season, on the Berlage in Amsterdam. A packed concert programme runs throughout the day, and is wide in scope — spanning from tango to classical, jazz, soul and folk performances. *Avenida Don Pedro de Mendoza 501, T 5533 5533, www.usinadelarte.org*

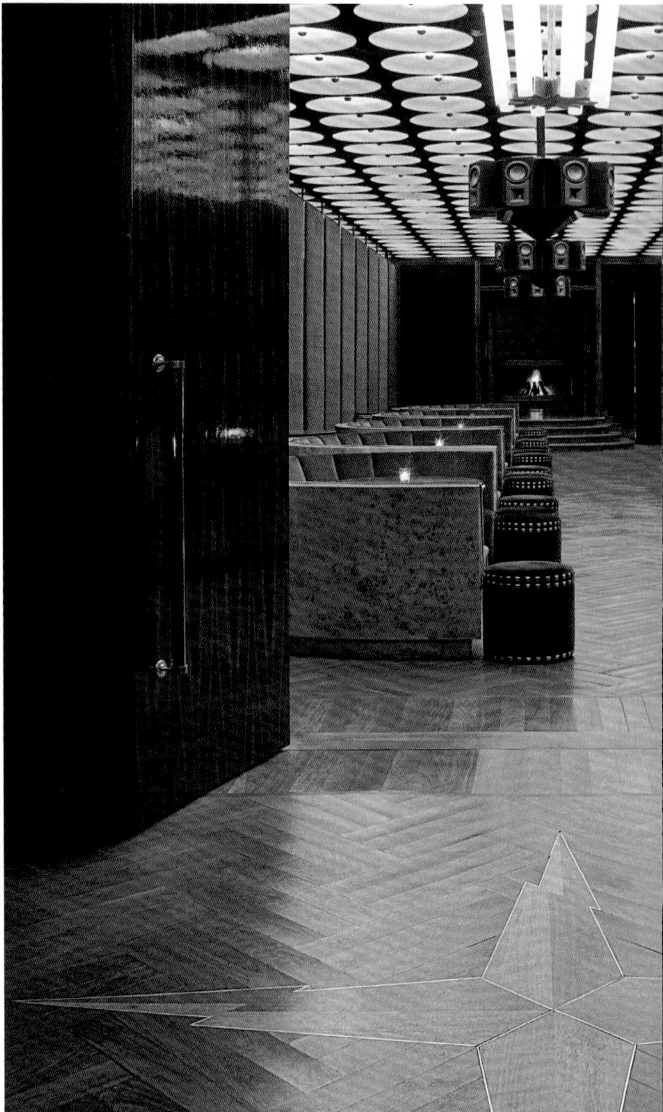

23.30 Isabel

Opened in 2009 and designed by BA style arbiter Juan Santa Cruz, Isabel is likely the most stylish bar in the world named after its founder's gran. Even empty, it's a sexy space, due to its curvy art deco booths, studded poufs and long mirror-backed bar, and it doesn't get any uglier when the models and actresses flounce in around midnight. The ceiling is a huge grid of circular light fittings inspired by the Whitney Museum's Breuer Building in New York; bulbs dim and flare in sync with the music. Grab a reassuringly expensive mai tai or champagne cocktail and head for the patio, where an open fire throws shadows on the marble walls. The hall-of-mirrors bathroom is stunning if you are sober, slightly disconcerting if not. The neo-Nordic menu at nearby Söder (T 4778 7025) is the perfect pre-Isabel dining plan.
Uriarte 1664, T 4834 6969,
www.isabelbar.com

URBAN LIFE

CAFÉS, RESTAURANTS, BARS AND NIGHTCLUBS

Argentina does not have much of a native gastronomy. But it does have meat sourced from grass-fed cows, salt and fire. BA's myriad *parrillas* (steakhouses) all work with these three simple elements, but naturally some do it with more flair, notably Elena's (Posadas 1086, T 4321 1200), Don Julio (Guatemala 4699, T 4832 6058) and La Carnicería (Thames 2317, T 2071 7199). Any other 'traditional' meal is more likely to be Italian. Try the spaghetti and meatballs at El Obrero (Agustín Caffarena 64, T 4362 9912), the house special at Pizzería Güerrin (Avenida Corrientes 1368, T 4371 8141) or *gelato* at Occo (Avenida Dorrego 1581, T 4777 9302). *Merienda* (essentially, afternoon tea) is enjoying a surge in popularity, and it doesn't get more stylish than at Ninina (see p025) or Farinelli (see p050).

However, a slew of young porteños is now enriching the scene, repurposing empty units (and often their own homes) into supper clubs (see p048) or speakeasy-style venues serving creative small plates (see p051). Meanwhile, modern restaurants at the forefront of experiments with the local gastronomy include Chila (see p042), Aramburu (Salta 1050, T 4305 0439) and El Baqueano (Chile 499, T 4342 0802). You don't have to wash all this down with malbec. The only thing more appealing than a cocktail at bars like Verne Club (Avenida Medrano 1475, T 4822 0980) and Shout Brasas & Drinks (Maipú 981, T 4313 2850) is the people mixing them. *For full addresses, see Resources.*

Fifi Almacén

In a neighbourhood oversubscribed with health food cafés, restaurant-deli-grocer Fifí Almacén stands out for its sleek, light-filled interiors. Designed by Horacio Gallo, it features a glossed pea-green floor, a white corrugated-zinc wall, Thonet chairs and a supersized communal table crafted from recycled petiribi wood. Repurposed fruit and vegetable crates are piled high with fresh produce and shelves fashioned from iron and eucalyptus display chichi cupboard supplies including jams, granola, housemade pickles and craft beers. Chef Luciano Combi whips up simple, seasonal fare, placing an emphasis on hearty salads and wraps. Brunch is served on weekends; the scrambled eggs with gravlax and hot cakes with organic honey are popular.
Gorriti 4812, T 2072 4295,
www.fifialmacen.com.ar

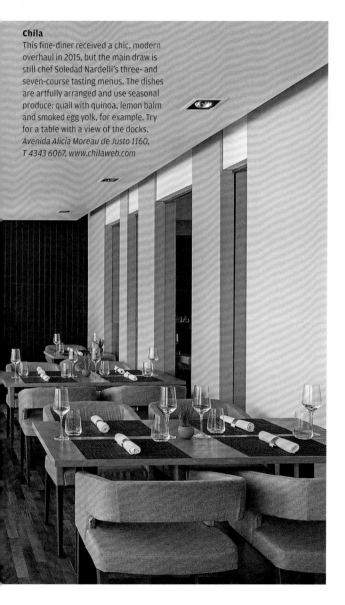

Chila

This fine-diner received a chic, modern overhaul in 2015, but the main draw is still chef Soledad Nardelli's three- and seven-course tasting menus. The dishes are artfully arranged and use seasonal produce: quail with quinoa, lemon balm and smoked egg yolk, for example. Try for a table with a view of the docks.
Avenida Alicia Moreau de Justo 1160, T 4343 6067, www.chilaweb.com

La Mar

This is the seventh in legendary Peruvian chef Gastón Acurio's chain of large, crowd-pleasing restaurants, but don't be put off; the food is the real deal. Local design duo Zunino + Grillo worked with Acurio's Lima-based team to devise the polished marine-inspired interiors within a restored 1920s building, installing lobster-pot light fittings by Patio Dorrego, while a mural evoking a fishing net covers the walls. The patio has a spacious central bar and custom-made wood furnishings by Fauna, and is the ideal spot for a Palermo Sour, which puts a Campari spin on the classic. From the kitchen come authentic dishes such as *tiradito* (fish carpaccio) 'cooked' in *leche de tigre* (a spicy citrus-based marinade), which sails out on a model fishing boat. *Arévalo 2024, T 4776 5543, www.lamarcebicheria.com.ar*

LAB Tostadores de Café

Speciality coffee purveyors are still a rare breed in Buenos Aires, which makes LAB a treat for those in search of a flat white. Co-owners Alexis Zagdanski and Federico Socin run this two-storey space, which includes an on-site roastery and cupping room. The neat ground-floor café serves carefully made brews, from pour over to espresso, as well as a short line in snacks, such as carrot cake and chocolate-chip cookies. Blends, perhaps Guatemalan or Ethiopian, change daily, and are chalked up on a blackboard. The duo collaborated with architect Marcelo Martínez for the interiors, which have an industrial feel, and feature a slim countertop, chestnut-hued polished concrete flooring, rough wooden cladding and exposed brickwork.
Humboldt 1542, T 4843 1790,
www.labcafe.com.ar

Frank's

This former banana warehouse has been converted into a pseudo-speakeasy that peddles prohibition-style consumption, and head barman Matías Granata's black-and-white letterboard is dominated by pre-1930s classics. It's not the only nod to the golden age of illicit drinking – you have to punch in a password in a phone booth to gain entry, a gimmick borrowed from Please Don't Tell, the acclaimed bolthole in Manhattan's East Village. Pull up a stool at the long wooden bar (above), behind which vintage cabinets display the libations, or sink into a leather armchair in one of the chandeliered living rooms as staff in waistcoats flit about. It would be a shame not to try the Cynar julep – Frank's interpretation of this Argentine artichoke-based aperitif is still very hard to beat. *Arévalo 1445, www.franks-bar.com*

Tegui

Often cited as one of the best restaurants in Latin America, this is the domain of chef Germán Martitegui. Set in a century-old townhouse plastered with graffiti by Nico Monti and Cavaio, the interior was created in collaboration with Horacio Gallo and is a skinny space featuring Knoll chairs, French lantern-style lighting, a lacquered ceiling and reclaimed-wood flooring, bookended by an open kitchen and a wine cellar that was fashioned from elm root, black glass and brushed steel. One side is flanked by a courtyard filled with banana plants. Order a cucumber martini and the seven-course tasting menu of mod Mediterranean and Argentine dishes, such as quail with tamale and figs, rabbit terrine with roast peaches, and black hake served with octopus.
Costa Rica 5852, T 5291 3333,
www.tegui.com.ar

I Latina

Siblings Santiago, Camilo and Laura Macías
launched their 'closed-door' restaurant in
2012 in a converted turn-of-the-century
townhouse. The fixed seven-course pan-
Latin American menu often includes treats
like coffee-braised pork loin or Colombian-
Caribbean-style ceviche with mango and
coconut; upgrade for the Argentine wine
pairings. Closed Sundays and Mondays.
Murillo 725, T 4857 9095

Farinelli

No knick-knacks, mismatched tableware or cupcakes – Farinelli is a café without the cliches. Co-owner Marina Bissone has devised a light-filled space, uncoloured save for the orange-red banquettes and the riffs on the company logo by designer Marina Pla; the chinaberry chairs are by Alejandro Sticotti of Net (see p081). Start your day the porteño way with a *cortado* (espresso served with a 'cut' of milk) and an authentic croissant (the local version, *medialunas*, are stickier and sweeter). At lunch, try a *milanesa* sandwich (breaded veal, which is very popular in BA) and a slice of wobbly cheesecake. The coffee is top-notch too. Farinelli has an outpost in Recoleta (T 4328 7998), and another in Palermo (T 4831 1600), opened in 2016. *Bulnes 2707, T 4802 2014, www.farinelli.com.ar*

Florería Atlántico

Pass through the florist to the wine shop, where a pair of bulky refrigerator doors form the entrance to this underground bolthole. It is co-owned by Renato 'Tato' Giovannoni, one of the best mixologists in town, and the inventive cocktail list was created by Sebastián Atienza, who helmed Milion (see p024) for many years, and was inspired by the nearby port, which saw a stream of European migrants arrive during the 19th century. The 'Italia' selection, for example, includes a granita made with Príncipe de los Apóstoles gin, Cynar, strawberry and mint. From the excellent, unfussy small-plates menu, order grilled octopus with potatoes and lemon. If it's packed, try sister bistro Brasero Atlántico (T 4393 7450), which is two doors down. *Arroyo 872, T 4313 6093, www.floreriaatlantico.com.ar*

Oporto

Following on from the success of his wine boutique Espacio G (T 4815 5242), Rodrigo Colombres established multitasking Oporto in 2014; it comprises a restaurant (above), deli, vinoteca and bar. Architect Horacio Gallo, who conceived the interiors for Fifi Almacén (see p041), designed the three-level space, set in an overhauled corner property in Nuñez, and the dining room features white tiling, wooden floors and black-lacquered Thonet chairs. Secure a pew on the terrace for the signature spritz (served with orange juice), before dinner cooked by Tegui (see p047) alumnus Tomás Di Lello, who sends out elevated Argentine classics, including *bondiola* (braised pork shoulder), using seasonal ingredients. The wine list consists of more than 500 labels. *11 de Septiembre 4152, T 4703 5568, www.oportoalmacen.com.ar*

INSIDERS' GUIDE

AGUSTIN YARDE BULLER AND MARTIN BOERR, DESIGNERS

When not working on collections for their hip eponymous label, design duo Martín Boerr (left) and Agustín Yarde Buller helm the Tupã concept store (see p093). 'There's a continual exchange of ideas that makes Buenos Aires so eclectic,' says Yarde Buller. 'It is not monotonous, which is why we love it.' A typical day might begin at Boûlan bakery (Ugarteche 3045) for *medialunas* before visiting a textile manufacturer at Palacio Barolo (Avenida de Mayo 1370). 'It represents the art nouveau epoch perfectly,' says Boerr.

Lunch staples are gnocchi with ricotta in the leafy courtyard of Museo Evita (Juan María Gutiérrez 3926, T 4800 1599) and quinoa salad from Farinelli (see p050), which they will eat in one of the city's green spaces: 'We really like Jardín Botánico (Avenida Santa Fe/Gurruchaga),' says Yarde Buller. Meetings are often conducted on the patio at Casa Cavia (see p030), after which they'll pop to Erdia (Avenida Quintana 34, T 4811 5105) to scout for accessories.

On an evening out, proceedings could well kick off at Butchers (Costa Rica 5863, T 4775 1872) with an aperitif. 'It's an intimate spot that serves excellent pork shoulder sandwiches.' Primavera Trujillana (Franklin D Roosevelt 1627, T 4706 1218) is also a regular haunt. 'We always order ceviche and a prawn *causa*.' A night out typically finishes up at Florería Atlántico (see p051), perhaps with a Julepe Ibérico: Serrano ham-infused gin with melon and basil. *For full addresses, see Resources.*

ART AND DESIGN

GALLERIES, STUDIOS AND PUBLIC SPACES

The modern BA scene grew out of Retiro's Calle Florida (see p062), nurtured by the Instituto Torcuato di Tella, which opened in 1958 and produced a generation of great artists, including Julio Le Parc, Antonio Berni, Edgardo Giménez and Marta Minujín. Di Tella is still prestigious today and has an exhibition space at the university in Nuñez (Avenida Figueroa Alcorta 7350, T 5169 7000), but recent years have seen a proliferation of hubs. The Distrito de las Artes was formalised in 2012, aimed at reviving San Telmo, Barracas and La Boca (see p058). High-profile galleries like Gachi Prieto (Aguirre 1017, T 4774 6656) and Nora Fisch (Avenida Córdoba 5222, T 156 235 2030), and upstarts Slyzmud (see p065) and Otero (Avenida Raúl Scalabrini Ortiz 1693), were enticed by Villa Crespo's empty sheds. The graffiti movement has also raised the city's profile, and Germán Martitegui even commissioned a coterie of street artists to add their signature to his upscale eaterie Tegui (see p047).

Import restrictions have forced contemporary designers to be resourceful, yet often with wonderful results. Cristián Mohaded (www.cristianmohaded.com.ar) used contrasting layers of scrap wood to create his elegant concave 'Bois' stool, and has produced a collection for Roche Bobois, and Alexandra Kehayoglou (see p066) creates extraordinarily tactile rugs from wool offcuts, and carpeted a fantastical catwalk for the Dries Van Noten 2015 show in Paris. *For full addresses, see Resources.*

RIES

'Alpina', the 2015 debut collection by RIES, is an exercise in geometry and proportion. The four almost skeletal pieces comprise a chair, table, desk and shelving unit, cast in solid iron and powder-coated in black, featuring surfaces of aqua-green Formica, copper and leather that contrast with the sharp framework. The young trio of Marcos Altgelt, Segundo Denegri and Tasio Picollo work out of a studio in Parque Chas; email hola@ries.com.ar to make an appointment. Argentina has a proud history of furniture design dating back to the late 1930s, when architects Kurchan and Ferrari Hardoy, as well as the Catalan Antonio Bonet, created the 'BKF' (Butterfly) chair for an apartment building they were working on in Buenos Aires. It has since become one of the most recognisable icons of the 20th century. *www.ries.com.ar*

Fundación Proa
When this industrial relic turned art space opened in 1996 in rundown La Boca, well outside the city's established zones of high culture, it was branded a bold, visionary project – code for 'crazy'. But the gamble paid off as it brought well-heeled locals to a rather touristy part of town that many had never visited. Housed in a harbour-front Italianate building first converted by Milan architects Giuseppe Caruso and Agata Torricella, and then renovated and reopened in 2008, Proa's headline shows (*Room 1: Beyond the White Walls*, part of Jeremy Deller's 'The Infinitely Variable Idea of the Popular', right) continue to draw the crowds. There's also a bookshop/ library, and a café/restaurant overseen by a team of young curators on the top floor that has a terrace offering superb views of this still shabby, soulful neighbourhood.
Avenida Don Pedro de Mendoza 1929, T 4104 1000, www.proa.org

Colección Fortabat

Uruguayan-born architect Rafael Viñoly created this museum for Amalia Lacroze de Fortabat, owner of one of the finest private art collections in Latin America. Viñoly is typically one for grand gestures, but this is comparatively understated. The exhibition halls are spread across six floors, two of which are underground. The building's upper levels are crowned by a claw-hammer-shaped steel-and-glass canopy overlaid with aluminium awnings that regulate natural light (the contrast with the subterranean rooms is striking). Look out for works by prominent Argentine artists, including Xul Solar and Kenneth Kemble ('Díptico No 1', opposite), and Andy Warhol's silkscreen portrait of Fortabat herself, which was commissioned in 1980. *Olga Cossettini 141, T 4310 6600, www.coleccionfortabat.org.ar*

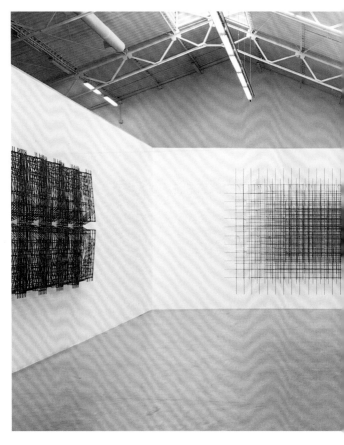

Ruth Benzacar

A key player in establishing a contemporary art scene in BA, Ruth Benzacar opened her gallery on chichi Calle Florida in 1965, and many of the young turks she championed are now some of the country's most highly regarded artists. Her daughter Orly picked up the mantle in the 1990s, by introducing talents such as the sculptor Adrián Villar Rojas, who represented Argentina in the 2013 Venice Biennale. After half a century, she broke from the traditional Retiro circuit in favour of a warehouse in Villa Crespo, which was reworked by Nicolás Fernandez Saenz. Its vaulted ceilings and polished concrete floors have provided the setting for a series of acclaimed shows by Liliana Porter, Jorge Macchi, Marina de Caro and Pablo Siquier ('Confort Psíquico', above). *Juan Ramírez de Velasco 1287, T 4313 8480, www.ruthbenzacar.com*

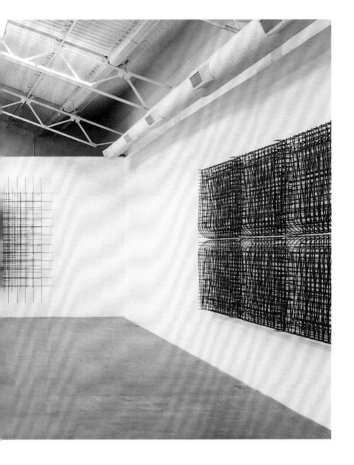

MACBA

Banker Aldo Rubino's gift to his hometown, MACBA opened in 2012 in San Telmo and shows off his vast hoard of geometric and abstract art. Local architects Vila Sebastian installed a glass facade to allow tantalising glimpses inside, and the raw concrete and ramps linking the four floors (above, with Gene Davis' *Blue-Violet*, top right) exude a brutalist feel that complements the works. Argentines are well represented, from Julio Le Parc, Manuel Espinosa, Gyula Kosice and Enio Iommi in the mid-20th century, to op artists Alejandro Puente and Ary Brizzi, up to present-day talents like Leila Tschopp, Natalia Cacchiarelli and Julia Masvernat. Next door is MAMBA (T 4361 6919), an old tobacco factory that houses BA's 7,000-piece modern art collection. *San Juan 328, T 5299 2010, www.macba.com.ar*

Slyzmud

Fusing their names and talent when they launched their gallery from a Villa Crespo storefront in 2011, Anglo-Argentine duo Natalia Sly and Larisa Zmud have curated a rich and eclectic mix of bimonthly shows ever since. On their roster are emerging and established Argentine artists, including Diego Gravinese, Vicente Grondona, Juan Stoppani and Miguel Mitlag. In 2015, the venture expanded into a satellite space a block away, which also puts on six annual exhibitions ('Sábanas Frescas' by Octavio Garabello, above). The former corner shop has been brilliantly reimagined by Nicolás Fernandez Sanz to create the illusion of a cube that juts out onto the sidewalk due to a cantilever and a painted triangle on the ground that defines a natural viewing area. *Bonpland 721, T 4857 0334, www.slyzmud.com*

Alexandra Kehayoglou
Hailing from a carpet-weaving dynasty,
Alexandra Kehayoglou has turned the
rug into a painterly art form – her huge
hand-loomed tufted-wool landscapes
evoke the pampas, mossy forests and
moonlit ponds. They're made using cast-
offs from her parents' factory. Email
hola@alexkeha.com to visit her atelier
(pictured) and to commission a piece.
T 156 915 2501, www.alexkeha.com

Floralis Genérica

Known as La Flor (The Flower), Eduardo Catalano's US$5m stainless-steel and aluminium kinetic work was inaugurated in 2002. Spanning 32m, it rests, lily-like, in a 44m reflecting pool, except at dawn, when its 'petals' open, and dusk, when they close. The nearby Canal 7 TV centre is an ensemble of Bauhaus-style boxes and sculptural pillars that's worth a look.
Plaza Naciones Unidas

FoLa

Inaugurated in 2015 by Gastón Deleau, who co-founded Buenos Aires Photo in 2005, FoLa occupies almost an entire block. The warehouse was remodelled by architects KLM and is distinctive for its white steel girders and polished concrete floors. It displays photography by Latin American artists, and launched with a series of images of Frida Kahlo and Diego Rivera shot by the Colombian Leo Matiz;

Santuario by Marcos López (above, centre) is from the growing permanent collection. Aficionados should also head to the smaller though arguably more influential Rolf Art (T 4804 4318). Its founder Flor Giordana Braun represents many eminent Argentine photographers, from Marcelo Brodsky and Adriana Lestido to the late Humberto Rivas. *Godoy Cruz 2626, T 5789 2773, www.fola.com.ar*

Faena Art Center

BA developer Alan Faena's Puerto Madero arts district is a cluster of hospitality (see p016), residential and cultural ventures, most of which inhabit the once-abandoned industrial sites. This exhibition space for large-scale works was unveiled in 2011 and sprawls across 4,000 sq m of the former engine room of Los Molinos, a grain mill at the turn of the last century. The witty agitprop installations of Cuban collective Los Carpinteros, as well as the graffiti-like abstractions of German Franz Ackermann (*Walking South* mural, above), are among the impressive pieces to have filled the two galleries. Running out of derelict buildings, Faena subsequently commissioned Foster + Partners to design The Aleph, a luxury apartment complex completed in 2012. *Aimé Paine 1169, T 4021 5555, www.faena.com*

ARCHITOUR

A GUIDE TO BUENOS AIRES' ICONIC BUILDINGS

Buenos Aires is a much younger city than Paris or London, but in some respects it feels way older. Architectural trends die hard here and as late as the 1940s wealthy families were treating themselves to neoclassical palaces and mock-Gothic follies. Nonetheless, you'll find many structures that were groundbreaking for their time too, including the Gaudí-esque Palacio Barolo (see p009), which was unveiled in 1923, and the huge 1934 art deco masterpiece that is the Mercado de Abasto (Avenida Corrientes 3247, T 4959 3400). Le Corbusier passed through BA in 1929 and planted the seeds of rationalism, but it wasn't until after the Peronist regime of 1946 to 1955 that modernism resurfaced under the auspices of the Di Tella collective (see p056). One important member was Clorindo Testa, whose crowning works include the Biblioteca Nacional (see p010), Banco Hipotecario (see p035) and the 1970 Hospital Naval (Avenida Patricias Argentinas 351), which resembles a baby-blue warship.

To find the 21st century, look to the city's fringes – to the Puerto Madero waterfront with its lustrous high-rise condos and office towers, notably Cesar Pelli's Torre YPF (see p015), or to the once-neglected 'hoods of Barracas and La Boca, where old warehouses and power plants have risen again as cultural centres. Following in the footsteps of Fundación Proa (see p058) is Usina del Arte (see p036), a concert hall hewn out of an electricity station.
For full addresses, see Resources.

Estadio Tomás Adolfo Ducó

Club Atlético Huracán has not won the Argentine league since 1973. However the Primera B side from the southern *barrio* of Parque Patricios are regarded as one of the big six in Argentine football, and play in a red-and-white art deco stadium that is second to none. You might recognise the ground, inaugurated in 1949, from the tracking shot in Juan José Campanella's 2009 Oscar-winning movie, *The Secret in Their Eyes*, in which the protagonists chase a Huracán supporter across the terraces. Fans are nicknamed *Quemeros*, or Burners, as the site was originally an incineration plant. Another stadium worth visiting is the central Estadio Arquitecto Ricardo Etcheverri (T 4431 8282), home to fellow B-leaguers Club Ferro Carril Oeste. *Avenida Amancio Alcorta 2570, T 4942 1965, www.clubahuracan.com.ar*

Puente de la Mujer

Winner of, among other awards, Worst Inauguration Day – 20 December 2001, when the government fell and violence swept across Buenos Aires – the 'Bridge of the Woman' has become one of BA's most beloved public structures. Designed by Spanish architect Santiago Calatrava, his first project in South America, and funded by Alberto L González (late owner of the Hilton Buenos Aires) to the tune of US$6m, the 170m-long pedestrian suspension bridge connects the west and east sides of the Puerto Madero dock. An inclined 39m-high pylon, intended to evoke the embrace of a duo mid-tango, supports a central section that rotates 90 degrees to allow water traffic to pass underneath. Take a stroll across it at sunset for one of the city's best views. *Dique 3*

Centro Cívico

The headline project in the rejuvenation of the southern suburb of Parque Patricios, an ex-industrial area, was unveiled in 2015. Foster + Partners' study in transparency for the city council, home to the mayor and 1,500 employees, set new environmental standards in the country. The undulating concrete roof, supported by columns at 8m intervals, cantilevers over the entrance and enables full-height glazing (the east and west facades are shaded by louvres), maximising natural light. The building recycles its own water, and only requires air-con for around half the year, relying on natural ventilation for the rest. Inside, there's an impressive four-storey atrium with staggered tiers of office space, and the open-plan layout means that there's a view of the park outside from most desks. *Uspallata 3150, Parque Patricios*

Automóvil Club Argentino

Like many of Buenos Aires' best buildings, the HQ of the Argentine Automobile Club looks out of place, a spartan intruder in a neighbourhood of overwrought embassies and showy mansions. Inaugurated in 1942, the stark, rectangular, 12-storey structure cloaked in dolomite was conceived by a hodgepodge design team associated with the rationalist movement, including Jorge Bunge and Antonio Vilar. The interior is more decorative, displaying murals and friezes by artists such as José Fioravanti and Alfredo Guido. In the museum on the first floor, many of the exhibits on show commemorate Juan Manuel Fangio, who was Argentina's greatest Formula One driver. Appropriately, the building faces Avenida del Libertador, itself a blur of speeding cars driven by would-be Fangios. *Avenida del Libertador 1850, T 4808 4000*

SHOPS

THE BEST RETAIL THERAPY AND WHAT TO BUY

Due to a lack of chains, shopping in Buenos Aires provides a series of delightful surprises. In its raft of independent boutiques, you are as likely to find yourself chatting to the designer as to a shop assistant. In Palermo Viejo alone, there are playful objets d'art in Tokonoma (see p082), tone-on-tone cotton shirts in Hermanos Estebecorena (El Salvador 5950, T 4772 2145), marine-inspired porcelain jewellery and ceramics by local makers in concept shop Patrón (Malabia 1644, T 4831 0351) and handwoven textiles and rugs in Elementos Argentinos (Gurruchaga 1881, T 4832 6299). A similar scene is also flourishing in the chic Botanical Gardens area. Avant-garde label Dubié (República de la India 3139, T 4807 3890) offers exquisite tailoring, and nearby Panorama (República de la India 2905, T 4806 0282) is BA's answer to Opening Ceremony.

Scout for modernist pieces by the likes of Eames and Miller in Midcentury, at its two outposts in San Telmo (Defensa 1181, T 5457 5009) and Palermo (Niceto Vega 5283, T 4300 8677). On Sundays, antique hunters can also cruise El Mercado de las Pulgas (Avenida Dorrego 1650). Finally, beware. It is only once you see the bespoke leather riding boots in La Casa de las Botas (Paraguay 5062, T 4776 0762) that you will realise how much you have always wanted a pair. Or visit the family-run cobbler Calzados Correa (Mario Bravo 750, T 4861 7344) in Abasto for prêt-à-porter and custom brogues. *For full addresses, see Resources.*

Net

Helmed by Alejandro Sticotti and Nicolas Tova, Net is an architecture firm that also produces a line of wooden furniture and homewares. The collection is crafted in a nearby workshop, and takes its cues from the elegant simplicity implicit in Nordic and Japanese design, melded with more rustic touches. We liked the stout form of the 'Taco' stool, which is fashioned from untreated alamo wood, and the 'Banco V', a slatted bench made from local petiribi, Brazilian lapacho or Mexican paraíso. More travel-friendly are the pine desktop-tidy boxes, and chopping boards. The spacious Palermo showroom, permeated with the scent of tropical timber, features cement floors and an outdoor patio, flanked with greenery, which hosts pop-up events.
Godoy Cruz 1740, T 4833 3901, www.sticotti.net

Tokonoma
Gallerist Oli Martínez collaborated with architect Clara Ortega to conceive this refined, two-level space, which features natural wood fixtures and arty wallpaper. The jewellery, pottery and homewares of more than 20 of the city's top artisans are on display; look for Silvana Lacarra's hand-painted dining table and brightly hued Colbo ceramics (T 260 442 0478). *Cabrera 5037, T 4831 8365*

El Ateneo Grand Splendid
This 1919 theatre by Rafael Peró and Manuel Torres Armengol reopened as a bookshop in 2000. Architect Fernando Manzone retained many of the original features, including the fluted columns, gilded tiers, boxes and the ceiling mural by artist Nazareno Orlandi. The English section doesn't live up to the space, and mostly consists of 1990s airport novels.
Avenida Santa Fe 1860, T 4813 6052

Juan Hernández Daels

Buenos Aires native Juan Hernández Daels studied at the Royal Academy of Fine Arts in Antwerp under the tutorship of Dries Van Noten and gained experience with Raf Simons before launching his namesake label in 2009. His flagship boutique, two storeys of whitewashed minimalism fitted with custom-made art deco-style railings and hangers, opened in 2015. Upstairs (above), precisely cut dresses, which often have an ethereal spin, in silk, organza and chiffon, share space with made-to-order samples with gentle pleats and laser-cut detailing. The ready-to-wear collection is displayed downstairs, and includes wool jackets with unusual tailoring, silk shirts and textured knitwear in block colour. A menswear range was unveiled in late 2016. *Libertad 1696, T 4815 4326, www.juanhernandezdaels.com*

Sabater Hermanos

Like many of the best independent brands, Sabater Hermanos does one thing and does it brilliantly. Here it's soap. The *hermanos* are siblings Sebastián, Martín, Eliana and Milagros, third-generation soap-makers who use the artisanal methods that their grandfather pioneered back in the 1930s to create contemporary, witty products. In store you'll find soaps perfumed with the essences of sandalwood, chocolate, mango, cedarwood, cinnamon and green tea; soaps shaped like golf balls, human figures, tiny flower petals and the alphabet; and soaps stamped with slogans like 'Don't wash your conscience' and 'Would you like to bathe with me?'. The walls are lined with grainy photos showing three Sabater generations at work and play. It's all good, clean fun.
Gurruchaga 1821, T 4833 3004,
www.shnos.com.ar

Not To Be Understood

Designer Jessica Trosman crafts garments that favour deconstructed forms and asymmetrical folds, which pair well with her more tailored leather jackets. This former mechanic's garage was refitted by local firm Net (see p081), who installed an Ekkehard Altenburger-inspired changing room (pictured) and a glass wall, which partitions the studio from the shop floor.
Humboldt 291, T 4857 6009

Monte

When Ricardo Paz and Belén Carballo opened this store/atelier in 1995, it was a defining moment in their love affair with antique textile art and furniture from the northern province of Santiago del Estero. Formerly a car workshop, this sprawling space exhibits high-end ethnic goods from flattering and unusual angles – witness the miniature chairs that hang from the ceiling. Some textiles date from the late 19th century and have abstract geometric designs; many, from the first half of the 20th century, have gorgeous floral motifs that display the influence of the Arts and Crafts movement as well as art nouveau. Contemporary pieces are handwoven using traditional methods. Only a fraction of the collection is on display; ask to see the storeroom upstairs for rarer treasures. *El Salvador 4656, T 4832 0516*

Federico Churba

Designer Federico Churba creates sleek products and furniture with an emphasis on sustainable luxury. The 'Saetas' tray (above) – the result of a collaboration with Patricio Lix Klett for the Argentine brand Solantú – is crafted from Patagonian wood sourced from a private forest and carved locally into irregular-shaped receptacles, which make for innovative fruit bowls. Churba's spacious store, fCH, fronts his studio and displays his entire collection, including signature pieces such as the 'Hanoi' lamp, which is made from a thin sheet of white Corian and inspired by a conical Vietnamese hat; and the slender and fluid 'Punto y Coma' floor light – an aluminium rod and orb globe suspended in mid-air by a counterweight system. *Paraná 1172, T 4813 6837, www.federicochurba.com.ar*

Fueguia 1833

Julian Bedel's budding BA perfume empire incorporates this gorgeous Recoleta store and outlets in Patio Bullrich (T 4814 7537) and Casa Cavia (see p031). The space is lush and theatrical, cloaked in dark velvet drapes, with lighting by ERCO and restored vintage chesterfields. The centrepiece is a long, altar-like table on which perfumes and candles are displayed atop recycled lenga and coihue wood boxes handcrafted in Patagonia. The scents are divided into eclectic categories. Some are inspired by the stories of Jorge Luis Borges, and others evoke Argentina's wild landscapes. All are unisex and all are blended from natural essences, using products including vellum, pink pepper, black tobacco, yerba maté and cedar. There's also a bespoke service. *Avenida Alvear 1680, T 4806 5619, www.fueguia.com*

Tupă

Local designers Martín Boerr and Agustín Yarde Buller (see p054) launched concept emporium Tupă in 2012. Inside you'll find their eponymous unisex label, defined by loose, asymmetrical silhouettes – cotton tunics and jackets with raw-edge hems, for example – a dusty, earthy palette and high-quality craftsmanship, as well as a small collection of other BA-based labels, like Schang-Viton and Maydi AZ, whose pieces are crafted from organic yarn. Tupă also displays acid-treated silver jewellery by Carolina Dutari, ceramic bowls by artist María Duffy and woollen blankets made by a knitting cooperative in Tucumán. Set within a restored 19th-century house, the spartan interiors feature concrete floors and artful arrangements of earthen pots.
Lafinur 3132, T 4806 7100,
www.tupatupa.com.ar

La Mersa
Established in 2006 by Fernando Samra
and Solange Bendjeunian, La Mersa (it
roughly translates as kitsch) sells design
objects and furniture from the 1950s to
the 1970s. The store moved to a groovier
showroom in 2011, and now there's even
more room for the Murano glass vases,
crystal ashtrays, demijohn table lamps,
and Scandinavian-style armchairs.
Nicaragua 4835, T 4771 2044

ESCAPES

WHERE TO GO IF YOU WANT TO LEAVE TOWN

One of the things porteños love about Buenos Aires is getting the hell out of it. The migration begins just after Christmas, when the routes are clogged to Mar del Plata on the Atlantic coast and Punta del Este in Uruguay. The latter is a kind of Sin City-on-Sea, a high-season blur of celebrities, branded parties and micro-thongs. Stay in hip La Posada del Faro (Calle de la Bahía, T +598 4486 2110), chef Francis Mallmann's Hotel Garzón (R9, Garzón, T +598 4410 2809) or Club Hotel Casapueblo (Punta Ballena, T +598 4257 8611), artist Carlos Páez Vilaró's labour of love. Dine on the day's catch with dressed-down heads of state and South America's Next Top Model at Parador La Huella (José Ignacio, T +598 4867 5432).

Closer to BA, and perfect for a quick getaway, are the grand estancias that dot the pampas. Among the retreats selling fresh air, real gauchos and as much horse riding as your thighs can handle are Estancia Villa María (Avenida Pereda, Máximo Paz, T 4815 0989), La Bamba de Areco (RP41/RP31, San Antonio de Areco, T 023 2645 4895) and Puesto Viejo (see p100). Or head north to Iguazú falls, and do the jungle in style at Posada Puerto Bemberg (Fundadores Bemberg, Puerto Bemberg, T 5236 9092). Most of Argentina's wine is produced in Mendoza (see p102), two hours' flight from the capital. Tour bodegas by day and sleep it off in a wine lodge like Cavas (Costaflores, Alto Agrelo, T 026 1410 6927). *For full addresses, see Resources.*

James Turrell Museum, Molinos, Salta
Purpose-built to exhibit installations by light-and-space artist James Turrell, this building is located 2,300m above sea level against the backdrop of the Andes, at the end of an hour-long drive along a dirt road. The man who made this happen is Donald Hess, art collector and owner of Estancia Colomé, the bodega in which the museum, a boxy red-brick structure designed by Turrell himself, is set. Opened in 2009, the museum covers 1,700 sq m and contains nine major works, including *Spread*, a 372 sq m walk-in environment made up of eerily suffused blue light, and *Unseen Blue* (above), in which a hole in the roof offers a sublime experience at dusk and dawn. Afterwards, stop off at the winery's tasting room to try the torrontés white.
Estancia Colomé, RP53 km20,
T 038 6849 4200, www.bodegacolome.com

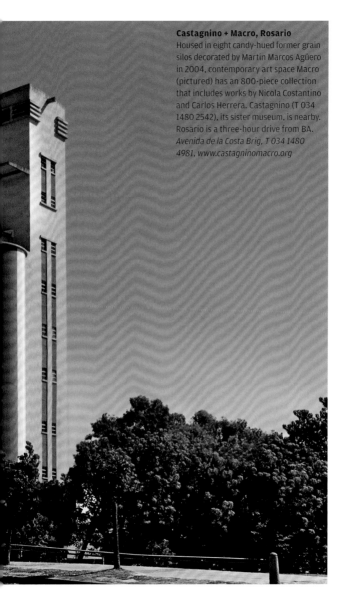

Castagnino + Macro, Rosario
Housed in eight candy-hued former grain silos decorated by Martin Marcos Agüero in 2004, contemporary art space Macro (pictured) has an 800-piece collection that includes works by Nicola Costantino and Carlos Herrera. Castagnino (T 034 1480 2542), its sister museum, is nearby. Rosario is a three-hour drive from BA. *Avenida de la Costa Brig, T 034 1480 4981, www.castagninomacro.org*

Puesto Viejo Estancia & Polo Club
Every weekend in the tournament season (November and December), Puesto Viejo hosts polo matches and, more importantly, post-game socials. Located near Cañuelas, 70km south of the city, this 220-hectare former cattle ranch now organises polo lessons, training and practice matches year-round. Stable facilities for the two-legged consist of 10 antique-furnished eclectic rooms (Rosie, above) in the 1918 lodge, which was remodelled by architect Sergio Morettini and co-owner Liliana Forrester-Baker. Watch a match from the infinity pool facing the pitch, or through binoculars from a hot-air balloon flight over the pampas. Talk tactics with horse owners, instructors and the players over farm-reared lamb at the communal table. *RN6 km83, Cañuelas, T 5279 6893, www.puestoviejoestancia.com.ar*

Casa de Uco, Mendoza

Situated along the Mendoza wine route, in the foothills of the Andes, Casa de Uco is a vineyard and resort designed by BA-based architect Alberto Tonconogy. Cast in glass and concrete, the 16-room property has a rustic-luxe feel; its interiors feature local sandstone, raw concrete, polished wood floors, leather sofas and cowhide rugs. Opt for one of the Laguna Suites, which have wide terraces and tubs with lake views (a man-made lagoon used for low-impact irrigation). The restaurant uses ingredients sourced from the kitchen garden in dishes like crispy sweetbreads with salsa *criolla*. Then there is the malbec, of course; enjoy a glass or two at the cellar's chrome Knoll table. The spa has a cedar-lined sauna and a treatment menu based on hydrotherapy. *RP94 km14.5, Vistaflores, T 026 1476 9831, www.casadeucoresort.com*

NOTES

SKETCHES AND MEMOS

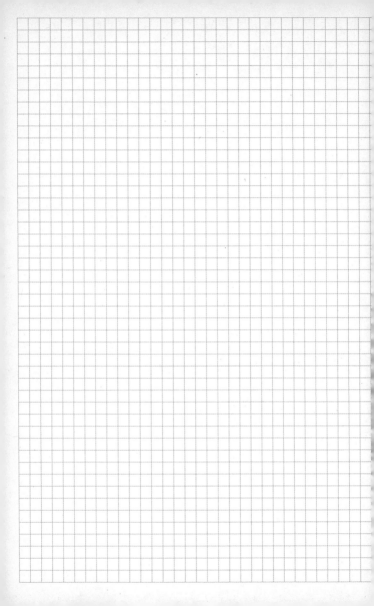

RESOURCES

CITY GUIDE DIRECTORY

HOTELS
ADDRESSES AND ROOM RATES

Algodon Mansion 016
  Room rates:
  Suite, from US$580
  Montevideo 1647
  T 3530 7777
  www.algodonmansion.com

Alvear Palace Hotel 016
  Room rates:
  double, from US$610
  Avenida Alvear 1891
  T 4808 2100
  www.alvearpalace.com

Casa de Uco 102
  Room rates:
  double, from US$485;
  Laguna Suite, US$725
  RP94 km14.5
  Vistaflores
  T 026 1476 9831
  www.casadeuco.com

Cavas Wine Lodge 096
  Room rates:
  double, from US$475
  Costaflores
  Alto Agrelo, Mendoza
  T 026 456 1748
  www.cavaswinelodge.com

Hotel Clásico 016
  Room rates:
  double, US$120
  Costa Rica 5480
  T 4773 2353
  www.hotelclasico.com

Club Hotel Casapueblo 096
  Room rates:
  double, from US$220
  Punta Ballena
  Punta del Este
  Uruguay
  T +598 4257 8611
  www.clubhotelcasapueblo.com

Hotel Dissors 024
  Room rates:
  prices on request
  Avenida General Paz 900
  T 4653 0314
  www.dissorshotel.com.ar

Faena 016
  Room rates:
  double, US$565
  Marta Salotti 445
  T 4010 9000
  www.faenahotelanduniverse.com

Fierro Hotel 022
  Room rates:
  double, from $205
  Soler 5862
  T 3220 6800
  www.fierrohotel.com

Four Seasons 016
  Room rates:
  double, US$635
  Posadas 1086
  T 4321 1200
  www.fourseasons.com/buenosaires

Hotel Garzón 096
  Room rates:
  double, from US$790
  (includes all meals)
  R9
  Garzón
  Uruguay
  T +598 4410 2809
  www.restaurantegarzon.com

The Haig 016
  Room rates:
  long-term stay, prices on request
  Humboldt 2060
  T 4772 3761
  www.haigba.com

WALLPAPER* CITY GUIDES

Executive Editor
Jeremy Case

Authors
Sorrel Moseley-Williams
Vanessa Bell

Art Editor
Eriko Shimazaki

Photography Editor
Rebecca Moldenhauer

Sub-Editor
Belle Place

Junior Editor
Emilee Jane Tombs

Contributors
Matt Chesterton
Sylvia Ugga

Interns
Catalina L Imizcoz
Georgie Emery
Electra Simon

Photo/Digital Assistant
Jade R Arroyo

Production Controller
Nick Seston

Wallpaper*® is a
registered trademark
of Time Inc (UK)

First published 2006
Revised and updated
2010, 2011 and 2013
Fifth edition 2016

© Phaidon Press Limited

All prices and venue
information are correct at
time of going to press,
but are subject to change.

Original Design
Loran Stosskopf
Map Illustrator
Russell Bell

Contacts
wcg@phaidon.com
@wallpaperguides

More City Guides
www.phaidon.com/travel

**Marketing & Bespoke
Projects Manager**
Nabil Butt

Phaidon Press Limited
Regent's Wharf
All Saints Street
London N1 9PA

Phaidon Press Inc
65 Bleecker Street
New York, NY 10012

Phaidon® is a registered
trademark of Phaidon
Press Limited

www.phaidon.com

A CIP Catalogue record for
this book is available from
the British Library.

Printed in China

ISBN 978 0 7148 7239 1

PHOTOGRAPHERS

Juan Hitters
Buenos Aires city view,
inside front cover
Biblioteca Nacional,
pp010-011
Edificio Kavanagh, p012
Torre IBM, p013
Edificio del Ministerio de
Salud, p014
Torre YPF, p015
Hotel Pulitzer, p017
Home, pp018-019
Moreno Hotel, p020
Palacio Duhau Park
Hyatt, p021
Fierro Hotel, pp022-023
Ninina, p025
Planetario Galileo
Galilei, pp026-027
Malba, pp028-029
Casa Cavia, p030, p031
8th Spa, pp032-033
Cementerio de la
Recoleta, p034
Banco Hipotecario, p035
Usina del Arte, p036, p037
Isabel, pp038-039
Fifí Almacén, p041

Chila, pp042-043
La Mar, p044
LAB Tostadores de Café,
p045
Frank's, p046
Tegui, p047
I Latina, pp048-049
Farinelli, p050
Florería Atlántico, p051
Oporto, pp052-053
Agustín Yarde Buller and
Martín Boerr, p055
Fundación Proa,
pp058-059
Colección Fortabat,
p060, p061
MACBA, p064
Slyzmud, p065
Alexandra Kehayoglou,
pp066-067
Floralis Genérica,
pp068-069
FoLa, p070
Faena Art Center, p071
Puente de la Mujer,
pp074-075
Centro Cívico, p076, p077
Autómovil Club
Argentino, pp078-079

Net, p081
Tokonoma, pp082-083
El Ateneo Grand Splendid,
pp084-085
Juan Hernández Daels,
p086
Sabater Hermanos, p087
Not To Be Misunderstood,
pp088-089
Monte, p090
Fueguia 1833, p092
Tupã, p093
La Mersa, pp094-095

Christopher Griffith
Estadio Tomás Adolfo
Ducó, p073

BUENOS AIRES

A COLOUR-CODED GUIDE TO THE CITY'S HOT 'HOODS

LA BOCA
This once down-and-dirty barrio is a hub of cheap eats and lively bars, and a riot of colour

SAN TELMO
BA's historic heart is going upmarket as boutique hotels move into reimagined buildings

PALERMO
A green lung that brings parks, polo, horse racing and a taste of the pampas to porteños

MICROCENTRO
Head here for the main museums, the presidential palace and grand architecture

PUERTO MADERO
This swanky modern dockland development is rapidly changing the face of the city

RECOLETA
Here is the BA of legend – a slice of Paris' 16th arrondissement in South America

PALERMO VIEJO
The pleasant home of the creative industries is chock-full of bars and restaurants

RETIRO
An interesting mix of beautiful boulevards and scruffy shanty towns across the rail tracks

For a full description of each neighbourhood, see the Introduction.
Featured venues are colour-coded, according to the district in which they are located.